AUGUSTA READ THOMAS

CHANT

for viola and piano

Augusta Read Thomas's *Chant* for violoncello and piano
(now withdrawn) was composed in 1989.
A new version, commissioned by cellist Kate Dillingham, was created in 2002
and given its premiere on 16 April 2002 at Merkin Concert Hall,
New York City by Ms. Dillingham with Blair McMillen at the piano.
This edition for viola and piano, based on the 2002 version,
has been transcribed by the composer.

The full work lasts 11 minutes.
The composer provides an option of ending the work after 9½ minutes.

The pianist should observe all pedal indications but may otherwise pedal freely.
All grace notes are to be played before the beat.

The original version of *Chant* (1989) was commissioned by Jeanne Kierman and Norman Fischer,
who premiered the work on 21 January 1992 at Rice University, Houston, Texas.
A recording of the original version is available on CD from Gasparo Records;
GSCD-349 0 2000 "American Music in the 1990's."

ED 4266
First Printing December 2005

ISBN 1-4234-0604-4

G. SCHIRMER, *Inc.*

DISTRIBUTED BY

7777 W. BLUEMOUND RD. P.O. BOX 13819 MILWAUKEE, WI 53213

for Jeanne and Norman Fischer

CHANT
for Viola and Piano

Augusta Read Thomas
(1990)

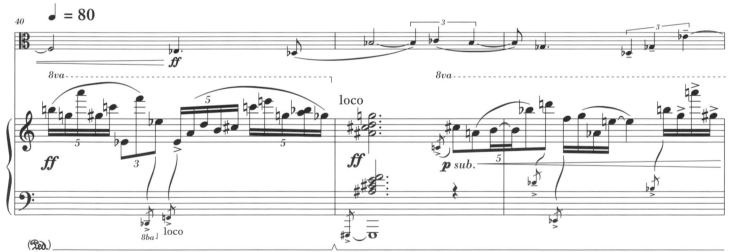

4

Majestic ♩ = 69

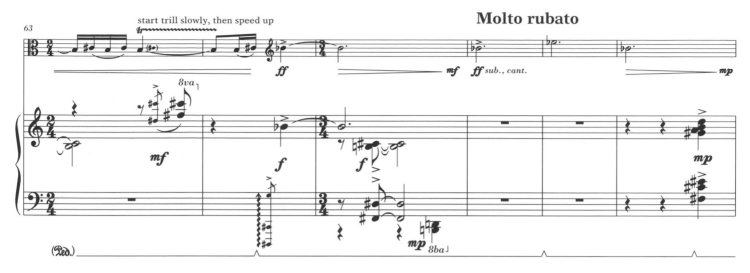

*The use of a mute for bars 72 through 98 is optional.

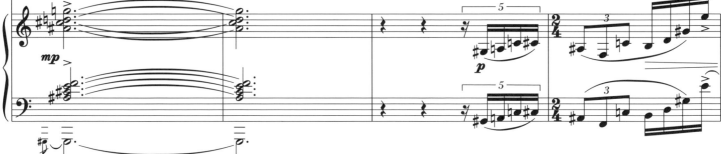

AUGUSTA READ THOMAS

CHANT

for viola and piano

viola

ED 4266
First Printing December 2005

ISBN 1-4234-0604-4

G. SCHIRMER, *Inc.*

DISTRIBUTED BY

HAL•LEONARD®
CORPORATION

7777 W. BLUEMOUND RD. P.O. BOX 13819 MILWAUKEE, WI 53213

Viola

for Jeanne and Norman Fischer

CHANT
for Viola and Piano

Augusta Read Thomas
(1990)

N.B.: Grace notes come before the beat.

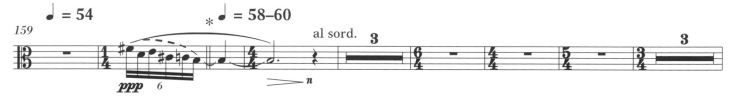

*The piece may, optionally, end here.

3

*The use of a mute for bars 72 through 98 is optional.

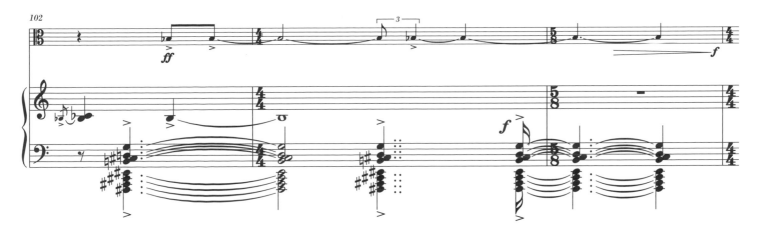

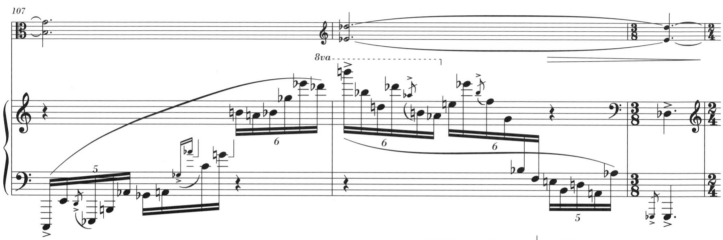

Molto rubato ♩ = 58

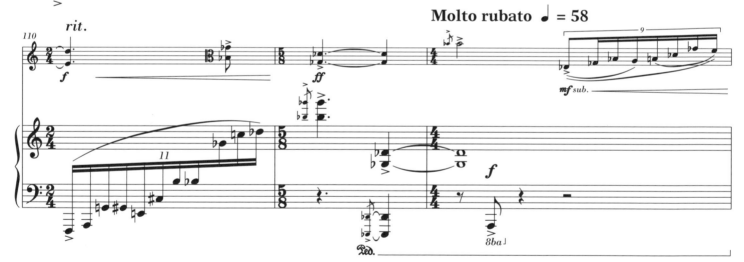

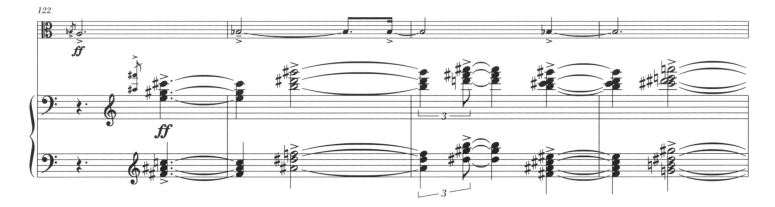

$\quad$ ♩ = 60

poco accel.

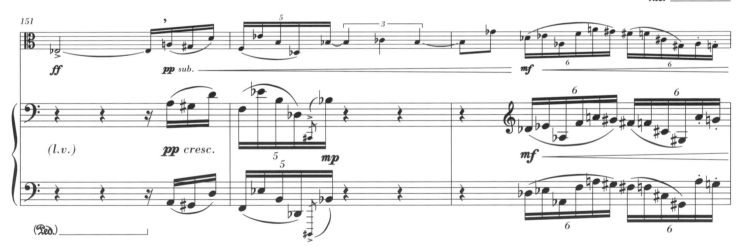

12

ca. 9½ minutes

*The piece may, optionally, end here.

ca. 11 minutes